DOUGH

Simple Contemporary Bread

DOUGH

Simple Contemporary Bread by Richard Bertinet

with photography by Jean Cazals

Kyle Cathie Limited

For Jo, Jack and Tom
With all my love

21st October 2009
54050000333047

Acknowledgements

To Sheila Keating, without whom I would not have got over the first hurdle, let alone past the finishing post; Kyle Cathie and her team for believing in this book; Jean Cazals for the amazing pictures and to Susanna Cook and the team at Allies for putting the jigsaw together.

To Tim White and John Warwick for making me a movie star (!); Sue Rowlands for props and croissants, Daniel Hopwood (www.danielhopwood.com), Model Catering (www.modelcatering.com), and Bill Amberg (www.billamberg.com) for letting us borrow their beautiful things and Amanda at Flirty (020 8960 9191) for trees and flowers.

To John Lister and Clive Mellums at Shipton Mill (enquiries@shiptonmill.com) for their advice and wonderful flour; Dan Lepard (www.danlepard.com) for his support and friendship; and AJ Tee at the French Croissant Company for his continued understanding.

To Alison, Sophie and Dan for looking absolutely fabulous and for getting out of bed for nothing; Joe, Alice, Eddie, Charlie and my boys for being our (guinea) pigs; and to Jane, Karl and Jackie for accommodating the overflow so graciously.

To Christine for her fabulous summer pudding recipe and marmalade and, together with Penny and Vicky, for proving my point that baking is fun; and to Kerry and Anna for being great friends and making the world around me run so smoothly while this book has been in the making.

Finally, to The Boss, for being there.

Richard is teaching and cooking at The Bertinet Kitchen in Bath. **www.thebertinetkitchen.com**

First published in Great Britain in 2005 by
Kyle Cathie Limited
122 Arlington Road, London NW1 7HP
www.kylecathie.com
This paperback edition first published in 2008

ISBN: 978 1 85626 762 5

A CIP catalogue record for this title is available from the British Library

10 9 8 7 6 5 4 3 2 1

Richard Bertinet is hereby identified as the author of this work in accordance with Section 77 of the Copyright, Designs & Patents Act 1988.

Text copyright © 2005 by Richard Bertinet
Photographs copyright © 2005 by Jean Cazals
Text layouts copyright © 2005 by Kyle Cathie Limited

Copy editor: Sophie Allen
Design: Susanna Cook and Anju Katharia at Allies
Indexer: Alex Corrin
Production: Sha Huxtable & Alice Holloway
Colour reproduction: Colourscan Pty Limited
Printed and bound in Singapore by Star Standard Industries Limited

contents

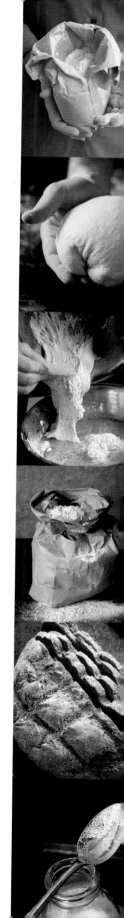

Companion: someone you share bread wit

I have been a baker most of my life and crazy about bread since I was a kid, but it wasn't until I started teaching people how to bake simple breads at home that I really appreciated what fun, and what a sense of achievement almost everyone experiences when they realise, for the first time, what can be done with some flour, yeast, water and a little salt. Breadmaking doesn't need to be daunting or mysterious and you don't have to be born a baker. Baking is for everyone. The aim of this book is simply to get you hooked on making bread. I'm not going to delve into the chemistry of breadmaking, analyse the properties of different flours, list masses of equipment or baffle you with complex techniques.

I look at it this way: do you need to know how a carburetor works to learn how to drive a car? No. Well nor do you need to immerse yourself in science to bake a wealth of wonderful breads. All the breads in this book are ones that I bake at home for my family and friends in my standard domestic oven, with my two young boys distracting me as much as they can. I teach them to the people who come to my bread classes, and I love the moment when the baking is finished and we all sit down with the breads we have made, some good cheese and ham and a glass of wine, and relax and enjoy the sense of achievement. I find that people really hate to break the spell – and nothing gives me more pleasure than to hear from them that they have baked the breads again successfully at home, and really enjoyed themselves in the process.

There is another reason for writing this book – the current climate of concern about the quality and safety of the food we eat, and the worry about additives, fat, sugar, salt and obesity. So much of what we eat is produced on a massive scale, with such a long and complicated chain of ingredients, suppliers and processes that many people are turning to smaller, artisan producers and farmers who can supply them with traceable food produced in simple, traditional ways, which they feel that they can have faith in. And what could be more trustworthy than your own bread, baked by your own hands in your own kitchen, using the best quality ingredients you can find? I will never forget the first time I visited a big industrial bakery in Britain, watching the loaves being mixed in minutes with the help of all kinds of 'improvers' and additives, and churned out on a massive scale – it gave me the shock of my life. I had never seen anything like it – it was so alien to everything I knew about bread.

I first fell in love with bread when I was very small. My uncle had a big bakery in Paris, my mother had at one time worked behind a bakery counter, and I was fascinated by the boulangerie in my home town in Brittany. When I was on holiday from school I used to go down there and stand on tip-toes so I could peer over the counter into the bakery itself. I could see the men working in their t-shirts, covered in flour, taking the bread out of the enormous ovens. The warm, yeasty smell was so seductive. When I was 12 or 13 years old I remember being asked in school, 'What do you

want to do when you are older?' and I replied that I wanted to be a baker. I had a friend whose uncle had a bakery, and he told me that I could come and work with them early one morning. I stayed with my friend in the house above the bakery, but I couldn't sleep for excitement. By midnight I had crept down – I couldn't keep away.

Baking was in my blood and, as soon as I could, I did my pre-apprenticeship, spending two weeks at school and two weeks and every weekend in the bakery. French bakeries are hard-working places but they have a magic too. There was a particular moment that I still miss, at around four o'clock in the morning, when the ovens were emptied, and there was no sound, except for the newly baked bread 'singing'. That's what we used to call the crackling sound that big loaves make when the crust breaks as it cools down – listen for yourself: when you hear it sing, that's when you know you have a good crust. In France of course, most people never bake their own bread because the tradition of buying it fresh, every day, is so strong. There is a bread for every occasion: a ficelle for breakfast, a baguette for lunch, a pain de mie for croque monsieur, a bigger pain de campagne or sourdough to put on the table or to keep and toast through the whole week. In France if there is no bread on the table at a mealtime it is a major catastrophe.

In Britain I knew there was a strong tradition of home breadmaking, but when I arrived here in 1988 I was shocked to find that very few people were bothering any more, not because there was a fantastic bakery around every corner, but because the staple diet was the sliced white loaf. There are over 200 varieties of bread available in the UK these days and we buy the equivalent of 9 million large loaves every day, but around 80% of the bread we buy is the sliced, wrapped sandwich loaf – and 75% of that bread is white. Most of the commercially made bread is produced using what is known as the Chorleywood Bread Process, invented in 1961 by the British Baking Industries Research Association at Chorleywood. The process is all about producing a cheap loaf, and it uses high–speed industrial mixers which produce the dough in minutes. Because the flour isn't necessarily the highest quality, and because you need to add as much water as possible to make the bread more commercially viable, pre-mixed 'improvers' and extra ingredients are added, such as emulsifiers, preservatives, fats, antifungal sprays and added enzymes, to make the dough softer, 'improve' the volume and prolong shelf life. As there is no real tradition of buying

bread daily in Britain, one of the first demands of any mass produced bread is that it will be able to sit on the shelf for up to a week without deteriorating – 'fresh?' – that's not my definition of fresh.

Of course there is a place for commercial sliced bread – to take as bait when you go fishing, or to make a bacon sandwich when you've got a hangover! – but if you make your own bread, you needn't worry about these suspicious ingredients because you are in control – and what do you need? Only flour, yeast, water and salt. No improvers, no enzymes, no stabilisers, emulsifiers or preservatives. And once you see the baking process in its natural, pure form then you can start asking questions to the people who make your bread commercially. Why do they need to add the contents of a chemistry set to your loaf? Skilled bakers can make bread on a large scale without bagfuls of additives, provided people are willing to pay a bit more for their bread – but there lie the two big issues: price and skill. Where have all the bakers gone?

Thankfully I think they are reappearing and, as they do, people are beginning to realise that it is worth paying a little more for the beautiful artisan breads they produce. At last there is a real surge of interest and excitement about breadmaking in this country, which is gathering pace. If I flash back to when I first arrived in Britain, I was amazed to find that in restaurants they seemed to serve bread almost as a canapé, before the meal, then it would be taken away, as if it was something separate from the rest of the food. However, over the last 10–15 years there has been a huge revolution in the way we think about food. And while at first, bread was overlooked in the new wave of excitement about restaurants and cooking, gradually chefs have begun to wake up to the idea that, as soon as someone sits down at the table, the arrival of a selection of breads with different flavours, shapes and textures immediately creates a welcoming and warm atmosphere and an expectation of more good things to follow. And as Britain's café culture continues to grow, sweet doughs, from croissants to brioche, have come into their own.

Of course what happens in restaurants influences the way we cook at home, and I quickly began to see that there was a real desire to bake, which was only held back by the idea that the process must be too complicated or time consuming; something to do on a special occasion with the kids, maybe, but not on a regular basis. That is when I began my breadmaking courses, teaching baking to a cross-section of people, from absolute beginners to those who had tried to make bread once, ended up with something that resembled a brick, and were so disillusioned they never tried again. I never dreamt that the classes would be so popular or so rewarding. I never get tired of seeing people's faces as their first bread comes out of the oven; they can't believe that they have made it themselves, without buckets of sweat and frustration.

People often say that those who like to bake and those who like to cook are made in different moulds. Well having worked both as a baker and a chef, I have never thought of baking and cooking as separate activities – to me baking bread is part of making a meal (it's also the best time to make dough, when the kitchen is warm from cooking) and I can't imagine dinner on the table without bread. Personally, I would love to see more chefs having a go at making their own bread. And every time I eat out, or talk to a chef about a combination of ingredients, I find myself thinking, 'I wonder what would be a good bread to go with that?' or, since bread is a natural carrier of flavours, 'How would those tastes work in a bread?'

Once you get into the habit of baking regularly, you can always have some bread part-baked in the freezer, ready to be finished off in the oven. Imagine giving your friends freshly baked fougasses, breadsticks or rolls when they come round to dinner; or the children coming home from school and asking for a chunk of fresh bread. Your bread.

bread tools

Hands – I always think it must be daunting to pick up a bread book that lists pages of expensive 'essential' equipment. The truth is that your hands are your most valuable tools – and really 'feeling' the dough is what breadmaking is all about.

Baking stone – in a traditional baker's oven, the bread is slid, using a wooden peel (or paddle), onto the hot brick floor, so that it starts to bake immediately underneath (it's the same principle as getting a grill-pan hot before you put on a steak). At the same time a steam injection system provides humidity which helps the crust to form. You can come close to creating a similar environment at home by getting a baking stone ready in the oven, and sliding your bread directly onto it. I have a piece of granite which stays in my oven all the time (you don't have to spend a lot of money – mine was an offcut that I found in a reclamation yard, and it's perfect). When I switch on the oven in the morning the stone is already in there so that by the time I come to bake it is thoroughly hot. Then, when I am ready to go, I just slide the loaves onto it, using a wooden peel or flat baking tray. You can also use a heavy baking tray, turned upside down so that it is flat.

Weighing scales – baking relies on exact measurements, so I weigh everything, including liquids, using digital scales, which is more accurate than relying on a level in a measuring jug. In many of the recipes which involve dividing the dough up into small rolls, baguettes, etc., I suggest that you weigh each piece of dough, and try to get them all equal – simply because, if you have lots of different sizes, some will bake quicker than others.

A mixing bowl – big enough to hold a kilo of dough. I use a stainless steel bowl.

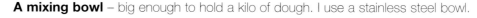

Tea towels – you only need a handful, for covering dough, and lining trays while it is resting. I use the same ones over and over again. I keep them in a separate drawer and don't wash them in between breadmaking sessions – the last thing I want is tea towels smelling of washing powder covering the dough. When you have finished making your bread, you just need to shake or brush the tea towels very well and let them dry. Over time the fabric becomes impregnated with natural yeasts and flavours, and the tea towels become an organic part of the whole breadmaking process.

Plastic scraper – this cheap little gadget is like an extension of my hand. I use it all the time: the rounded end to mix the dough, to help turn it out from the mixing bowl so that it comes out easily in one piece, without stretching, and to scrape up and lift pieces of dough from the work surface. The straight edge can be used for cutting and dividing the dough. It's also fantastic for scraping the ice from your windscreen in winter! If you don't have one you can always use a large, flat wooden spoon, or even a plastic credit card you received free in the post!

Razor blade – for slashing the tops of loaves and rolls to help create more crusty edges. Of course you can use a sharp knife, but the razor blade fitted into a handle, known as a lame, is the traditional baker's 'pen' which you use to put your 'signature' on your bread, and it does the job swiftly and cleanly.

Wicker proving basket – not essential at all, just a traditional and lovely thing designed to hold round loaves while they are proving. The wicker makes an ideal container because it allows the air to circulate around the dough and let it breathe – and you can clean the basket and use it to serve the bread afterwards.

Wooden peel – this is really useful for transferring your proved bread to your baking stone or tray in the oven. If you don't have one, you can use a flat-edged baking tray, or if you only have a tray with a lip, turn it upside down.

Water spray – the kind you use for spraying houseplants is perfect for misting the oven with water as you put in bread that needs to develop a good crust and colour. This, combined with the baking stone, really helps to recreate the atmosphere of a bakery.

Timer – don't assume you will remember to take the bread out at the right time! I have three timers all on the go, otherwise I know I will get caught out when one of the kids distracts me or the phone rings.

Soft brush – mine is like a little handbrush you might use for sweeping. I keep it on my work bench for brushing off flour. Don't wash down your bench until the end of your breadmaking session. Just scrape off any pieces of dough with your scraper, brush away any unwanted flour, and then when you are completely finished, you can wash down your surface thoroughly with soap and water.

ingredients

Flour – all I want to say about flour is: use proper, good-quality strong bread flour, the best quality you can afford. One of the questions I am always asked in my classes is where do I buy mine from, as once people have made bread successfully I find that when they get home they want to reproduce everything they have done exactly, using identical ingredients. Well, I buy most of mine from Shipton Mill in Tetbury, Gloucestershire, who offer an amazing range of flours from all over the world, for use in every style of baking. Many of the flours are organic, and all of them are stone-ground and untreated. Alternatively, Leckford Estate Strong White Four, or Canadian Strong White Flour, both from Waitrose, are very good.

Yeast – I am tempted to say only use fresh yeast and avoid dried, but it is worth having some dried yeast in the cupboard for that moment when you have an overwhelming urge to bake and you find you are out of fresh. One of the things that seems to amaze people is how easy it is to use fresh yeast. I don't believe in adding sugar and warm water to yeast to 'activate it' before using it – inevitably I find people add water that is way too hot, which will leave you with a sticky mess, and anyway none of this is necessary. All you need to do is rub the yeast into the flour using your fingers, just as if you are making a crumble. If you do have to resort to dried yeast, treat it in exactly the same way.

Water – I use tap water in all my recipes (at room temperature). If you have a water filter even better. Frankly I don't see any benefit in using bottled water, which has probably been sitting inside glass for a few years – I like to drink it, yes but, for breadmaking, I wouldn't bother.

Salt – use fine sea salt, preferably organic. I know there is a lot of angst about the salt content in bread these days, yet the absurd thing is that it is often the very people who are worrying who are also giving their children bags of salt-laden crisps to eat. All I can say is that I happily give my children fresh home-made bread to eat, but they don't have crisps or any other processed food full of hidden salt. Salt in bread stabilises the fermentation and helps the colour and flavour. In some parts of the world, like Tuscany, they traditionally eat bread made with no salt, but to me it is like eating a steak that hasn't been seasoned properly. If you want to reduce the level of salt, of course you can, but the results won't be as good.

bread talk

Every baker has his own terms and expressions. These are mine:

Working the dough – the kneading technique that most people are taught in Britain is quite different from the one we use in France, which is all about getting air and life into the dough. So, instead of using the word kneading (which sounds too harsh) I prefer to talk about working the dough (see page 24).

Resting – this is the time when the worked dough is left, usually for about 1 hour, covered with a tea towel, in a warm, draught-free place, during which time it will rise to around double its volume and develop its structure, while the flavour matures. 'Where is this warm, draught-free place?' 'Warm' is after all quite a loose term which might suggest different things to different people. What I mean by warm is the ambient temperature in my kitchen after I have had the oven on since early morning (around 25–30°C). You can use a microwave (turned off, of course), or a kitchen cupboard – but I would avoid using an airing cupboard, as is often suggested, as it will dry out the dough too much, likewise the top of your cooker, which will also be too hot. If you do feel that your dough is drying out as it rests, move it away from any obvious heat source and spray some water onto the top of the tea towel that covers it.

Folding – usually in Britain I find people are taught to 'knock back' the dough to take the air out of it once it has rested. I hate that term – it suggests you need to bash the dough to bits, but you should be much more gentle with it. I just turn the dough upside down, then fold the outside edges of dough in on themselves a few times, pressing down each time, and turning the dough around to form it into a ball. Folding and pressing down the dough is also the moulding technique I use to mould the dough into different shapes.

Proving – this is the time when the dough is left again, after it has been moulded, or shaped into loaves, rolls, etc. Again it will expand to around just under double its volume – this will usually take around 1 hour. The reason I say 'just under' double is that, until you get a feel for baking it isn't always easy to guage that moment when the volume of your dough has doubled, and you will get better results if you slightly under-prove your bread, than if you over-prove it.

Baking – it may sound obvious, but bread is 'baked' not 'cooked'. I often hear people talking about 'cooking' bread, which to me is as weird as hearing someone saying they're going to 'bake' a piece of beef.

Ferment – some bakers use the term 'levain', which means the same thing – a piece of dough that has been left at least 4–6 hours to 'ferment' and which adds character and flavour and lightens the finished bread. A few of the breads use a 'poolish', which is just the name for a particular style of ferment.

working the dough

resting

fermenting

proving

folding

baking

Colour Chart – when you start baking and read things like 'bake until golden brown' it doesn't necessarily mean that much – so I thought I would help by giving you a colour chart, showing the various shades the crust will go through as you continue to bake.

Note: Of course this only really applies to breads made with white, olive or sweet dough as brown or rye bread will necessarily be darker.

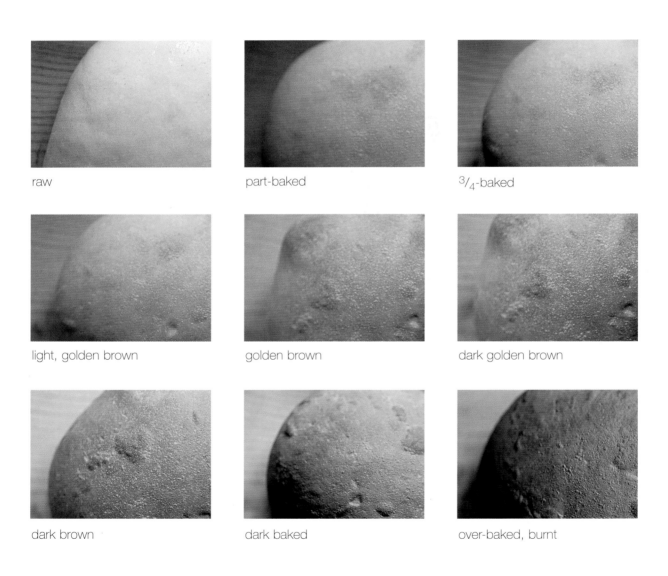

raw   part-baked   ³/₄-baked

light, golden brown   golden brown   dark golden brown

dark brown   dark baked   over-baked, burnt